STICK MAN

By Julia Donaldson

Illustrated by Axel Scheffler

ALISON GREEN BOOKS

Stick Man lives in the family tree
With his Stick Lady Love and their stick children three.

One day he wakes early and goes for a jog.
Stick Man, oh Stick Man, beware of the dog!

"A stick!" barks the dog.
"An excellent stick!
The right kind of stick
for my favourite trick.

"I'll fetch it and drop it,
and fetch it – and then

"I'll drop it and fetch it
and drop it again."

"I'm not a stick! Why can't you see,
I'm Stick Man, *I'm Stick Man*,
   I'M STICK MAN, that's me,
And I want to go home to the family tree!"

A notice says:

DOGS MUST BE KEPT ON THE LEAD.

At last the game's over, and Stick Man is freed.

He sets off for home with a hop and a twirl.
Stick Man, oh Stick Man, beware of the girl!

"A stick!" cries the girl
with a smile on her face.
"The right kind of Pooh-stick
for winning the race!

"Has everyone got one? Get ready to throw."
It's 1, 2, 3 - into the river they go!

"I'm not a Pooh-stick! Why can't they see,
I'm Stick Man, *I'm Stick Man*, I'M STICK MAN, that's me,
And I'm heading away from the family tree!"

Stick Man is floating. He floats on and on.
Stick Man, oh Stick Man, beware of the swan!

"A twig!" says the swan. "This twig is the best!
It's the right kind of twig to weave into my nest."

"I'm not a twig! Why can't they see,

I'm Stick Man, *I'm Stick Man*, I'M STICK MAN, that's me,

And I long to be back in the family tree."

The nest is deserted, and Stick Man is free.

He drifts down the river and sails out to sea!

He tosses and turns, till the frolicking foam
Washes him up on a beach far from home.

Here comes a dad with a spade in his hand.
Stick Man, oh Stick Man, beware of the sand!

"A mast!" yells the dad. "An excellent mast!

"Hooray! There's a flag on our castle at last."

"I'm not a mast for a silly old flag,

Or a sword for a knight . . .

or a hook for a bag.

I'm not a pen!

I'm not a bow!

I'm not a bat . . .

or a boomerang – no,
I'm . . ."

Stick Man, oh Stick Man, beware of the snow!

Here comes a boy in a warm woolly scarf.
"An arm for my snowman!" he says with a laugh.

"I'M NOT AN ARM! Can nobody see,
I'm Stick Man, *I'm Stick Man*, I'M STICK MAN, that's me!

"Will I *ever* get back to the family tree?"

Stick Man is lonely, Stick Man is lost.
Stick Man is frozen and covered in frost.
Stick Man is weary. His eyes start to close.
He stretches and yawns and lies down for a doze.

He can't hear the bells, or the sweet-singing choir . . .

Or the voice saying, "Here's a good stick for the fire!"

Stick Man is lying asleep in the grate.

Can anyone wake him before it's too late?

He dreams of his kids and his Stick Lady Love,

Then suddenly wakes.
    What's that noise up above?
It starts as a chuckle,
    then turns to a shout:
"Oh-ho-ho ho-ho . . . I'm STUCK!
    Get me OUT!"

A Stuck Man? *A Stuck Man?*
    Now who could that be?
"Don't worry!" cries Stick Man.
    "I'll soon set you free."

A scratch and a scrape and
    a flurry of soot.
A wiggle, a jiggle, and –
    out pokes a foot!
A shove and a nudge,
    a hop and a jump . . .

And Santa falls into the room with a thump!

"Stick Man, oh Stick Man, you excellent friend!
Thanks! Thanks a million! Thanks without end!"

Then Stick Man helps Santa deliver the toys
To fast-asleep girls . . .

and to fast-asleep boys.

Faster and faster they fly through the snow,
Till Santa says, "Only one chimney to go!"

Stick Lady's lonely. The children are sad.
It won't feel like Christmas without their Stick Dad.
They toss and they turn in the family bed.
But what is that clattering sound overhead?

Someone is tumbling into their house.
Is it a bird, or a bat, or a mouse?
Or could it . . . yes, could it just possibly be . . .

"I'm Stick Man, *I'm Stick Man,*
I'M STICK MAN, that's me!
And I'm sticking right here
in the family tree."

For Adélie

First published in the UK in 2008 by
Alison Green Books
An imprint of Scholastic Children's Books
Euston House, 24 Eversholt Street
London NW1 1DB
A division of Scholastic Ltd
www.scholastic.co.uk
London – New York – Toronto – Sydney – Auckland
Mexico City – New Delhi – Hong Kong
This paperback edition published 2016

PB ISBN: 978 1 407170 71 8

1 3 5 7 9 8 6 4 2